Acknowledgements

Thanks to Alda, Karole, Lisa and Mahesh for their inputs.

Dotted-text was created using Hershey Text - an Inkscape Extension.

Illustrations were created on Inkscape - free, open source software.

Book design & layout was done on Scribus - free, open source software.

A crow sat on a tree to eat lunch.

A crow sat on a tree to eat lunch.

A crow sat on a tree to eat lunch.

A fox saw the food and wanted it.

A fox saw the food and wanted it.

A fox saw the food and wanted it.

He tried to trick the crow.

He tried to trick the crow.

He tried to trick the crow.

He asked the crow to sing a song.

He asked the crow to sing a song.

He asked the crow to sing a song.

The crow knew the fox's trick.

The crow knew the fox's trick.

The crow knew the fox's trick.

If she opens her beak, the food will fall.

If she opens her beak, the food will fall.

She put the food under her feet.

She put the food under her feet.

She put the food under her feet.

Then she sang out, "Caw, caw, caw!"

Then she sang out, "Caw, caw, caw!"

Then she sang out, "Caw, caw, caw!"

The fox walked away sadly.

The fox walked away sadly.

The fox walked away sadly.

The wise crow enjoyed her meal.

The wise crow enjoyed her meal.

The wise crow enjoyed her meal.

www.ingramcontent.com/pod-product-compliance
Lightning Source LLC
Chambersburg PA
CBHW040043100526
44583CB00027BA/3325